Spelling Made Easy

Key Stage 1

AGES 6-7

Author Su Hurrell

LONDON • NEW YORK • MUNICH • MELBOURNE • DELHI

Certificate

Congratulations to

....
(write your name here)

for successfully finishing this book.

GOOD JOB!

You're a star.

AGES 6-7
Key Stage 1

Date

....

LONDON, NEW YORK, MUNICH,
MELBOURNE, and DELHI

DK UK
Editor Jolyon Goddard
Managing Art Editor Richard Czapnik
Producer, Pre-production Francesca Wardell
Producer Christine Ni

DK Delhi
Editor Rohini Deb
Art Editor Dheeraj Arora
Assistant Art Editor Kanika Kalra
DTP Designer Anita Yadav
Managing Editor Soma B. Chowdhury

Published in Great Britain in 2014 by Dorling Kindersley Limited
80 Strand, London WC2R 0RL

Copyright © 2014 Dorling Kindersley Limited
A Penguin Random House Company
10 9 8 7 6 5 4 3 2 1
001—196492—July/2014

A CIP catalogue record for this book is available from the British Library.
ISBN 978-1-4093-4943-3

Printed and bound in China by L. Rex Printing Co., Ltd.

Discover more at
www.dk.com

Contents

This chart lists all of the topics in the book. When you complete each page, stick a star in the correct box. When you've finished the book, sign and date the certificate.

FACTS

One of the spellings for the long **a** sound is **a_e**. The vowels are split by a consonant, as in the word **late**. The letter **e** is written at the end of each word.

Complete these words and draw lines joining them to the right picture.

c _ k _

sk _ t _

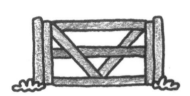

g _ t _

t _ p _

Complete the following sentences.

I h _ t _ smelly fish.

 I think football is a good g _ m _ .

Do you know my n _ m _ ?

 Twins can look the s _ m _ .

4

Another spelling for the long **a** sound is **ai**. This spelling appears in the middle of words, as in tr**ai**n.

Complete these words and draw lines matching them to the right picture.

tr_ _ _n

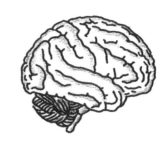

spr_ _ _n

r_ _ _n

br_ _ _n

Complete the following sentences.

 I ran for the tr_ _ _n.

Little Red Hen planted a gr_ _ _n of wheat.

 I lost a coin down the dr_ _ _n.

I went to Sp_ _ _n for a holiday.

★ The long "a" sound

FACTS

When the letters **ay** are together in a word, they are used for the long **a** sound. This spelling appears at the ends of words

Add **ay** to the end of each of these words and then read the words.

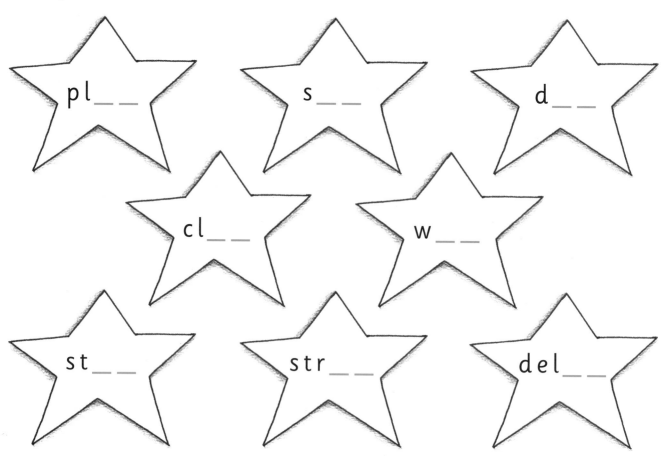

All the words above rhyme. Make up your own funny rhyming poem below.

....

....

....

....

....

> The days of the week all end in the letters **ay**, which are used for the long **a** sound.
>
> Mon**day** → Wednes**day** → Fri**day** → Sun**day**
>
> Tues**day** → Thurs**day** → Satur**day**
>
> Learn to spell the days of the week, as you will often need to write them.

Complete this rhyme. The first day of the week has been done for you.

Solomon Grundy

Born on Monday,

Christened on .... ,

Married on .... ,

Took ill on .... ,

Worse on .... ,

Died on .... ,

Buried on .... ,

This is the end of Solomon Grundy.

Answer these questions about Solomon Grundy.

On what day was he born? ....

On what day was he married? ....

On what day did he die? ....

FACTS

One of the spellings for the long **i** sound is **i_e**. The vowels are split by a consonant, as in the word **line**. The letter **e** is written at the end of each word.

Complete these words and draw lines joining them to the right pictures.

n_ n_

w_ n_

p_ p_

k_ t_

f_ v_

l_ n_

Complete the following sentences.

I had a r_ d_ on my b_ k_.

I had a big b_ t_ of an apple.

Another spelling for the long **i** sound is **igh**.

Complete this silly rhyme.

In the middle of the n _ _ _ t,

When the Moon was br _ _ _ t,

Two scary beasts got up to f _ _ _ t,

Ugh! What a s _ _ _ t.

They gave me a fr _ _ _ t.

Quick! Quick! Let's turn out the l _ _ _ t.

Draw pictures of the two scary beasts.

What are their names? Give the beasts names with the long **i** sound in them.

9

FACTS

When the letters **ie** are together in a word, they are used for the long i sound.

Add **ie** to make these
words on the pie rhyme.

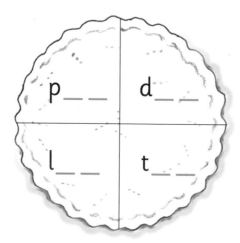

p _ _ _   d _ _ _

l _ _   t _ _ _

The letter **y** by itself can also be used for the long i sound.
Make these words rhyme by adding **y**.

fl_   dr _   sk _   cr _   sp _

All the words above rhyme. Make up your own funny rhyming poem below.

....

....

....

....

Complete these sentences using the words from the box below.

fly	sky	cry

I .... when I hurt myself.

A .... nearly landed on my beans.

In a storm, the .... is dark and cloudy.

FACTS

Usually, when the letters **ee** or **ea** are together in a word, they are used for the long **e** sound.

Complete these words and join them to the right pictures. If you are unsure which spelling to use, write the word both ways to see which looks right.

b _ _

thr _ _

tr _ _

b _ _ ns

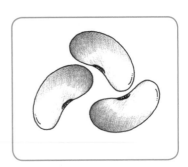

fl _ _ s

r _ _ ding

b _ _ ch

t _ _ ch

Same letters, different sounds

FACTS

The letters **ea** are used for two different sounds, the long **e** sound, as in b**ea**ch, or the short **e** sound, as in h**ea**d.

Draw a (ring) around the words below that have the long **e** sound in the middle.

head	tea	tread	beaver	thread
dead	reach	team	meat	spreading
bean	bread	teacher	reading	breathing

FACTS

One of the spellings for the long **o** sound is **o_e**. The vowels are split by a consonant, as in the word **note**. The letter **e** is written at the end of each word.

Complete the words below and join them to the right pictures.

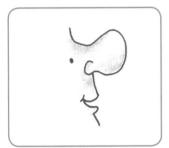

b _ n _

c _ n _

r _ s _

n _ s _

sm _ k _

st _ n _

Complete these sentences using the words from the box below.

| rose | bone | mole | hole |

My dog loves to chew on a ....

A .... is a beautiful flower.

I am a .... and I like to live in my ....

The long "o" sound

FACTS

Another spelling for the long **o** sound is **oa**.

The letters **ow** can sometimes also make the long **o** sound, as in sn**ow**.

Draw a line to join each word to the right picture.

coat

boat

throat

goat

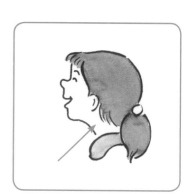

Complete these sentences using the words from the box below.

| snow | slow | low | show |

The sign at the crossroads says, "Go ....!"

I will .... you my football cards.

I have to bend .... to do up my laces.

In winter, we sometimes have ....

One of the spellings for the long **u** sound is **u_e**. The vowels are split by a consonant, as in **flute**. The letter **e** is written at the end of each word.

The letters **ew** and **ue** are also used for the long **u** sound.

Draw a line to join each word to the right picture.

cube

tube

tune

mule

Complete these sentences using the words from the box below.

| flew | blue | grew | glue | clue | chew |

In summer, the sky is ....

The detective found an important ....

My little puppy finds it hard to .... a bone.

The little robin .... away when I went too close.

The .... I used was really sticky.

Jack's beans .... and ....

Crossword

FACTS

Learning word families, such as **fly**, **high** and **pie**, will help your spelling and rhyming.

Complete this crossword. Use the picture clues to help you.

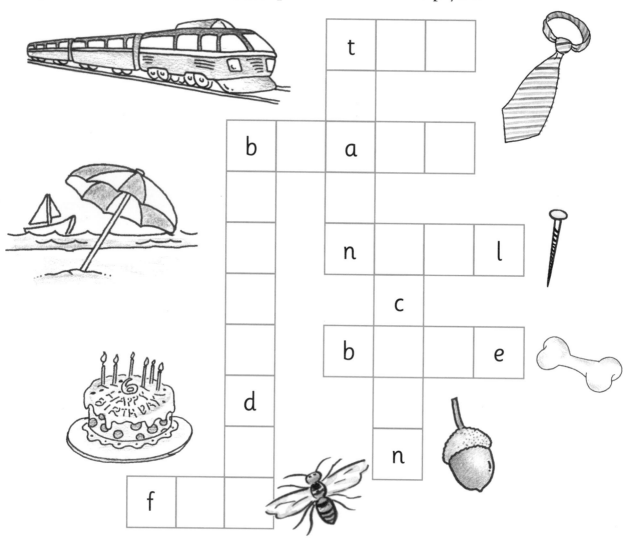

Draw a (ring) around the word in each line that does not rhyme.

light	fit	fright	tight	kite
mane	train	plane	cap	cane
goat	coat	throat	not	note
fly	high	pie	my	fine
sea	bee	then	three	tree

Spelling practice ★

Writing out words is the best way to learn their spellings.

Look at each word carefully. Say it. Cover it up with your hand. Write it.
Check it. Were you right?

are	....	before	....
about	....	could	....
after	....	another	....
find	....	because	....
good	....	have	....
must	....	right	....
old	....	your	....
want	....	very	....
mother	....	father	....
should	....	school	....

Write the five sentences that are read out to you.
Listen, think and then write.

....

....

....

....

....

FACTS

English words never end in the letter **v**. The letters **ve** together are used for the short **v** sound, as in ha**ve**.

The words in the box end with the letters **ve**. Use them to complete the sentences below. You can use the words in the box more than once.

| mauve | live | cave | love | give | leave | move |

"Ugh! Ugh! I will never .... away and .... my

.... !" shouted the huge, scary .... monster.

"I .... to .... in this dark ....

and I .... to .... you a FRIGHT!"

Draw a picture of the scary monster. Give him two names that rhyme.

....

Sometimes, words end with the letters **le**, as in bub**ble**.

Add **le** to complete these words and then draw a line from each word to the correct picture. Say each word and listen to the **le** sound.

bund_ _

cand_ _

tab_ _

bott_ _

sadd_ _

pudd_ _

scribb_ _

jugg_ _

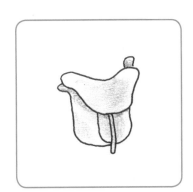

FACTS

Sometimes, different letters can be used for the same sound.
For example: **ow** as in c**ow** and **ou** as in cl**ou**d.

Read the words in the box. Write the words with **ou** under the cloud and those with **ow** under the cow.

cloud   sound   down   frown   cow   now   owl
gown   mouse   house   found   brown   around   out

ou

....

....

....

....

ow

....

....

....

....

Complete these sentences using the words from the box below.

house   cloud   How   cow   mouse   brown   towel   owl

The .... ran up the clock in the nursery rhyme.

A big, black .... hung over my ....
when there was a storm.

.... are you?

I saw a big, ... in a field.

When I found a baby .... , I wrapped it in an old ....

FACTS

> A **suffix** is a group of letters that can be added to the end of a **root word**.
> For example: **ing**, **er**, **en**, **ed**, **est** and **y** are all suffixes.
>
> **Remember**: if a word ends in **e**, take it away before you add a suffix.

Add a suffix to each of these root words and write the new word.

smile + ing = ...

brave + er = ...

fine + est = ...

like + ed = ...

take + en = ...

nose + y = ...

Complete these sentences. Use the words you have written above.

Ali's cup is finer than Jo's, but my gold cup is the .... of all.

I did not like waiting in the queue, but I .... the roller coaster.

I hate having to smile for a photo, but I like .... at other times.

Dad told me not to take my new boots to school, but it was too late! I had already .... them.

FACTS

The word that you add a suffix to is called the **root word**.

Write the root word for each of these words.

smiling

waving

....

....

diving

writing

....

....

dancing

hiding

....

....

Look at each root word above, cover it and write it down again.

....

....

> When a **root word** ends in a short vowel and a consonant, **double** the last letter before adding a suffix, such as **ing**, **ed**, **er**, **en**, **est** or **y**.
> For example: **hop + ing = hopping**

Finish these word sums.

shop   +   ing   = ...

slip   +   ed   = ...

fun   +   y   = ...

sad   +   est   = ...

fat   +   en   = ...

mud   +   y   = ...

run   +   ing   = ...

hot   +   est   = ...

sun   +   y   = ...

Remember: Look   Say   Cover   Write   Check

Can you spell these words?

after	....	bird	....
many	....	more	....
some	....	home	....
ask	....	work	....
would	....	open	....
boy	....	she	....
every	....	may	....
any	....	help	....
best	....	left	....
back	....	these	....

Write the sentences that are read out to you.
Listen, think and then write.

....

....

....

....

....

....

The letters **ck** and **k** are used for the same sound. How do you know which one to use? You have to look at the word and ask yourself, "Does that look right?"

Which word in each pair looks right? Write the correct word on the dotted line.

ticket tiket	sok sock	clock clok

....

roket rocket	duck duk	fork forck

....

frok frock	chik chick	lock lok

....

The letter **k** always needs the letter **c** to stand between it and a **short vowel** sound, as in ne**ck**. The letter **k** can stand alone after a **long vowel** sound, as in li**ke**. It can also stand alone after some consonants, as in wa**lk**.

Complete these words.

pa_ _

ki_ _

ba_ _

po_ _ et

so_ _

lo_ _

bri_ _

lo_ _ et

Complete these words.

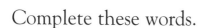

for_

tal_

wal_

wee_

li_e

bi_e

spea_

bea_

> Sometimes, the letters **wa** sound like **wo**, as in **wa**tch, and the letters **wor** sound like **wer**, as in **wor**d.

The Wonderful Witch changes how the letter **a** sounds after the letter **w**. She can make the letters **wa** sound like **wo**.

Complete these words.

s _ _ n

s _ _ tter

_ _ tch

_ _ _ sp

_ _ nd

_ _ _ shing

The Wonderful Witch can also cast a spell to make **wor** sound like **wer**. Write the missing words into these sentences. Choose from the box below.

| word   worm   world   worship |

I would love to travel around the .... in a rocket.

A .... is very slippery and wiggly, but it has no legs!

Shh! Don't say a .... or you will wake up the baby.

Some people go to a temple or a church to ....

The following words are used to ask a question:

why   when   what   which   where   who

Here are some funny riddles. Fill in the missing question words.

.... did the chicken cross the road? *(To get to the other side.)*

Knock! Knock! .... is there? *(Aunt.)*
Aunt .... ? *(Aren't you ready yet?)*

.... is a door not a door? (........................ it is a jar.)

.... would you find the Andes? *(On the ends of your armies.)*

.... would you find two apples that are the same? *(On a pair tree.)*

.... goes up when rain comes down? *(An umbrella.)*

.... is yellow and swings through the trees? *(Tarzipan.)*

.... is the most dangerous city in the world? *(Electricity.)*

Don't get in a muddle

There are many spellings for the sound **air**, as in ch**air**.
For example: **are**, **ere**, **ear** and **air**.

There are many spellings for the **or** sound.
For example: **or**, **oor**, **aw**, **au** and **ore**.

Complete these sentences using the words in the box below.

chair	there	care	bear

I sat on a broken ....

I have a very old teddy ....

"Go over .... ," the teacher said.

Walking in the rain is fun. I don't .... if I get wet.

Draw a line joining each word to the correct picture.

door

draw

daughter

claw

snore

saw

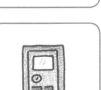

FACTS

Some words that are spelled differently sound the same but mean different things. For example: **which** and **witch** sound the same but have different meanings.

Underline the words in the sentences below that sound the same but don't mean the same thing and then write both words.

I am over here. I couldn't hear you calling.

....

I can see their coats. They are over there.

....

An elephant has a trunk and two tusks, too.

....

Where are you are going? You can't wear that hat!

....

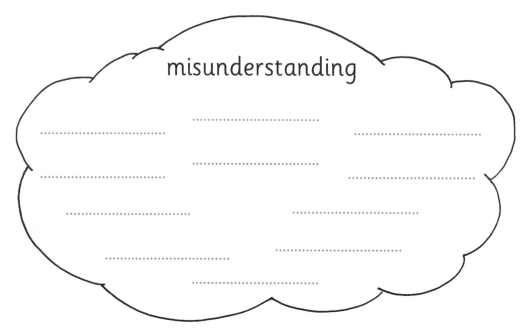

How many small words can you make from this large word?

misunderstanding

Colours of the rainbow

Colour words and other descriptive words enrich writing skills.

Finish these sentences with the correct colour word.

Roses are ....

The sky is ....

Corn is ....

The grass is ....

I like a nice juicy ....

Violet is another word for ....

Night is ....

Snow is ....

A tree trunk is ....

An elephant is ....

Colour each of the balloons
using a pen that matches
the colour word inside it.

orange

yellow

black

red

blue

purple

white

grey

green

brown

More spelling practice

Remember: Look   Say   Cover   Write   Check

Can you spell these words?

their	....	year	....
there	....	under	....
then	....	woman	....
where	....	tell	....
what	....	keep	....
who	....	sit	....
them	....	own	....
how	....	let	....
us	....	little	....
yes	....	which	....

Write the sentences that are read out to you.
Listen, think and then write.

....

....

....

....

....

Answer section with parents' notes

Key Stage 1
Ages 6–7

This eight-page section provides answers and explanatory notes to all the activities in this book, enabling you to assess your child's work.

Work through each page together and ensure that your child understands each task. Point out any mistakes your child makes and correct any errors in spelling. (Your child should use the handwriting style taught at his or her school.) As well as making corrections, it is very important to praise your child's efforts and achievements.

At the end of this section, there is a glossary that includes all the key terms covered in this book.

★ The long "a" sound

FACTS One of the spellings for the long **a** sound is **a_e**. The vowels are split by a consonant, as in the word **late**. The letter **e** is written at the end of each word.

Complete these words and draw lines joining them to the right picture.

c**a**k**e**

sk**a**t**e**

g**a**t**e**

t**a**p**e**

Complete the following sentences.

I h**a**t**e** smelly fish.

I think football is a good g**a**m**e**.

Do you know my n**a**m**e**?

Twins can look the s**a**m**e**.

The activities on this page focus on the spelling **a_e** for the long **a** sound. Ask your child to complete the words with the long **a** sound and to match them to the right pictures. Encourage him or her to say the words aloud.

The long "a" sound ★

FACTS Another spelling for the long **a** sound is **ai**. This spelling appears in the middle of words, as in tr**ai**n.

Complete these words and draw lines matching them to the right picture.

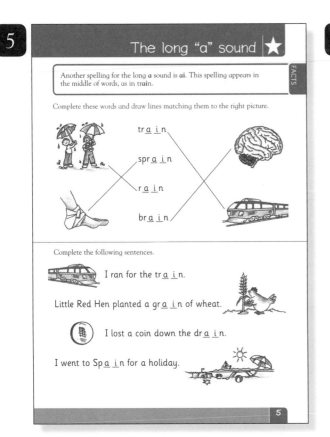

tr**ai**n

spr**ai**n

r**ai**n

br**ai**n

Complete the following sentences.

I ran for the tr**ai**n.

Little Red Hen planted a gr**ai**n of wheat.

I lost a coin down the dr**ai**n.

I went to Sp**ai**n for a holiday.

This page introduces the idea that more than one vowel combination can be used for one sound. Encourage your child to look for words with the **ai** spelling pattern when reading books and other printed material.

★ The long "a" sound

FACTS When the letters **ay** are together in a word, they are used for the long **a** sound. This spelling appears at the ends of words

Add **ay** to the end of each of these words and then read the words.

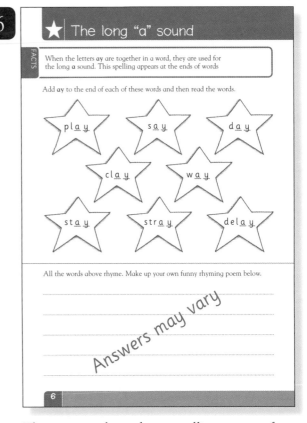

pl**ay**   s**ay**   d**ay**

cl**ay**   w**ay**

st**ay**   str**ay**   del**ay**

All the words above rhyme. Make up your own funny rhyming poem below.

Answers may vary

This page explores the **ay** spelling pattern for the long **a** sound. Rhyming is introduced and your child is encouraged to create rhymes using the words on the page.

The days of the week ★

FACTS

The days of the week all end in the letters **ay**, which are used for the long **a** sound.

Monday → Wednesday → Friday → Sunday
↘ Tuesday → Thursday → Saturday

Learn to spell the days of the week, as you will often need to write them.

Complete this rhyme. The first day of the week has been done for you.

Solomon Grundy

Born on Monday,

Christened on _____Tuesday_____ ,

Married on _____Wednesday_____ ,

Took ill on _____Thursday_____ ,

Worse on _____Friday_____ ,

Died on _____Saturday_____ ,

Buried on _____Sunday_____ ,

This is the end of Solomon Grundy.

Answer these questions about Solomon Grundy.

On what day was he born? _____Monday_____

On what day was he married? _____Wednesday_____

On what day did he die? _____Saturday_____

7

It is important that your child learns to spell the days of the week. He or she should complete the fun rhyme Solomon Grundy and then answer the short comprehension questions about the rhyme at the end of the page.

★ The long "i" sound

FACTS

One of the spellings for the long **i** sound is **i_e**. The vowels are split by a consonant, as in the word line. The letter **e** is written at the end of each word.

Complete these words and draw lines joining them to the right pictures.

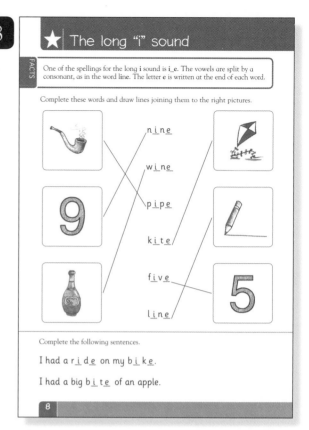

n i n e

w i n e

p i p e

k i t e

f i v e

l i n e

Complete the following sentences.

I had a r i d e on my b i k e.

I had a big b i t e of an apple.

8

These activities focus on the spelling **i_e** for the long **i** sound. Your child completes the words by adding **i_e** and then matches the words to the pictures. He or she may like to continue this activity by making other new words.

The long "i" sound ★

FACTS

Another spelling for the long **i** sound is **igh**.

Complete this silly rhyme.

In the middle of the n i g h t,

When the Moon was br i g h t,

Two scary beasts got up to f i g h t,

Ugh! What a s i g h t.

They gave me a fr i g h t.

Quick! Quick! Let's turn out the l i g h t.

Draw pictures of the two scary beasts.

What are their names? Give the beasts names with the long **i** sound in them.

Answers may vary

9

This page introduces the spelling **igh** for the long **i** sound. There is a silly rhyme for your child to complete. He or she can then draw the pictures of the two scary beasts and think of names that include the long **i** sound.

★ The long "i" sound

FACTS

When the letters **ie** are together in a word, they are used for the long **i** sound.

Add **ie** to make these words on the pie rhyme.

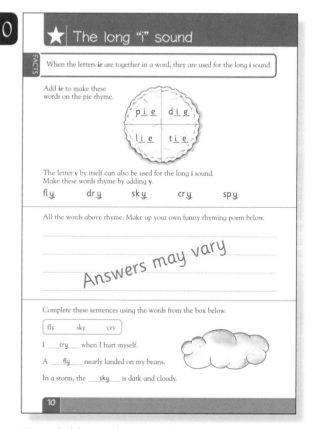

p i e   d i e

l i e   t i e

The letter **y** by itself can also be used for the long **i** sound. Make these words rhyme by adding **y**.

fl y   dr y   sk y   cr y   sp y

All the words above rhyme. Make up your own funny rhyming poem below.

Answers may vary

Complete these sentences using the words from the box below.

fly   sky   cry

I ___cry___ when I hurt myself.

A ___fly___ nearly landed on my beans.

In a storm, the ___sky___ is dark and cloudy.

10

Your child completes words with the spelling patterns **ie** and **y** for the long **i** sound and then writes a rhyme. Understanding how rhymes are created will help him or her when spelling new words and remembering them.

The long "e" sound ★

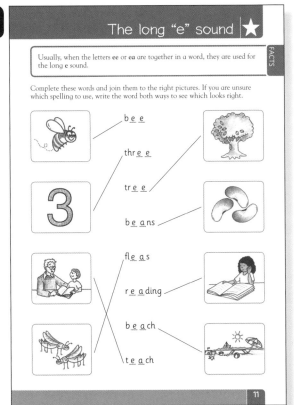

FACTS

Usually, when the letters **ee** or **ea** are together in a word, they are used for the long e sound.

Complete these words and join them to the right pictures. If you are unsure which spelling to use, write the word both ways to see which looks right.

b e e

thr e e

tr e e

be a ns

fle a s

r e a ding

b e a ch

t e a ch

11

The activity on this page introduces the spelling patterns **ee** and **ea** for the long e sound. This page reinforces the need for your child to look as well as listen when remembering spellings.

★ Same letters, different sounds

FACTS

The letters **ea** are used for two different sounds, the long e sound, as in beach, or the short e sound, as in head.

Draw a ring around the words below that have the long e sound in the middle.

head   (tea)   tread   (beaver)   thread

dead   (reach)   (team)   (meat)   spreading

(bean)   bread   (teacher)   (reading)   (breathing)

12

This page reinforces using of the same spelling for different sounds – in this instance, **ea** for both the long and short e sounds. Your child needs to say all the words but only circle those with long e sound, as in be**a**ch.

The long "o" sound ★

FACTS

One of the spellings for the long o sound is **o_e**. The vowels are split by a consonant, as in the word note. The letter e is written at the end of each word.

Complete the words below and join them to the right pictures.

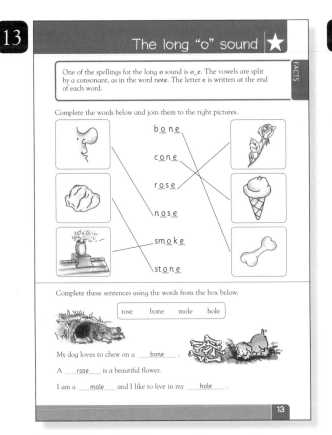

b o ne

c o ne

r o se

n o se

sm o ke

st o ne

Complete these sentences using the words from the box below.

| rose | bone | mole | hole |

My dog loves to chew on a ___bone___ .

A ___rose___ is a beautiful flower.

I am a ___mole___ and I like to live in my ___hole___ .

13

The activities on this page focus on the spelling **o_e** for the long o sound. Your child completes the words by adding **o_e** and joins the words to the pictures. He or she then completes the sentences in the second activity.

★ The long "o" sound

FACTS

Another spelling for the long o sound is **oa**. The letters **ow** can sometimes also make the long o sound, as in snow.

Draw a line to join each word to the right picture.

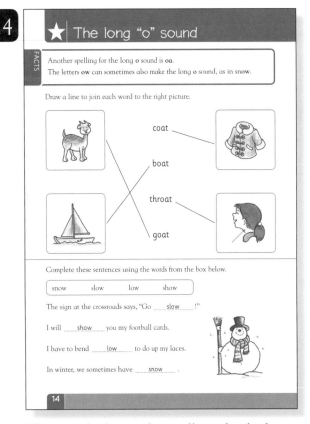

coat

boat

throat

goat

Complete these sentences using the words from the box below.

| snow | slow | low | show |

The sign at the crossroads says, "Go ___slow___ !"

I will ___show___ you my football cards.

I have to bend ___low___ to do up my laces.

In winter, we sometimes have ___snow___ .

14

This page looks at other spellings for the long o sound – **oa** as in coat and **ow** as in snow. Encourage your child to look for words with these spelling patterns when reading.

The long "u" sound ★

FACTS
One of the spellings for the long **u** sound is **u_e**. The vowels are split by a consonant, as in **flute**. The letter **e** is written at the end of each word. The letters **ew** and **ue** are also used for the long **u** sound.

Draw a line to join each word to the right picture.

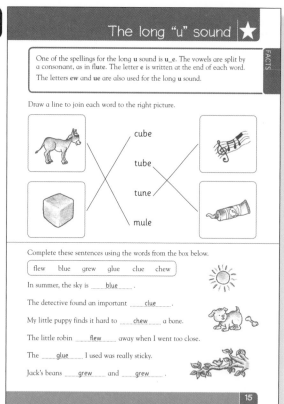

cube

tube

tune

mule

Complete these sentences using the words from the box below.

flew   blue   grew   glue   clue   chew

In summer, the sky is _____blue_____ .

The detective found an important _____clue_____ .

My little puppy finds it hard to _____chew_____ a bone.

The little robin _____flew_____ away when I went too close.

The _____glue_____ I used was really sticky.

Jack's beans _____grew_____ and _____grew_____ .

15

This page looks at the spelling patterns for the long **u** sound: **u_e**, **ew** and **eu**. Encourage your child to both look at and say the words. You can reinforce these spellings by making illustrated lists of additional words.

★ Crossword

FACTS
Learning word families, such as **fly**, **high** and **pie**, will help your spelling and rhyming.

Complete this crossword. Use the picture clues to help you.

	t	i	e
b	e	a	c	h
	i		i
	r	n	a	i	l
	t		c
	h	b	o	n	e
	d		r
	a		n
f	l	y

Draw a ring around the word in each line that does not rhyme.

light	(fit)	fright	tight	kite
mane	train	plane	(cap)	cane
goat	coat	throat	(not)	note
fly	high	pie	my	(fine)
sea	bee	(then)	three	tree

16

On this page, there is a crossword to complete and an exercise in which your child has to find the words that do not rhyme. Encourage him or her to say the words aloud and also to look carefully at how they are spelled.

Spelling practice ★

FACTS
Writing out words is the best way to learn their spellings.

Look at each word carefully. Say it. Cover it up with your hand. Write it. Check it. Were you right?

are	are	before	before
about	about	could	could
after	after	another	another
find	find	because	because
good	good	have	have
must	must	right	right
old	old	your	your
want	want	very	very
mother	mother	father	father
should	should	school	school

Write the five sentences that are read out to you. Listen, think and then write.

When / I was / very little, / I could not / reach / the shelf.

I like / Saturday best / because / I can / lie in bed.

Some nights / when it is / very dark, / I can see / the full moon.

On Monday, / I had / to push / my bike / back to / the house.

In summer, / people go to / the beach / for a holiday.

17

Encourage your child to complete carefully the Look, Say, Cover, Write and Check activity. Read the dictation and then repeat slowly, pausing at the marks shown above. Encourage him or her to listen, think and then write.

★ The "ve" ending

FACTS
English words never end in the letter **v**. The letters **ve** together are used for the short **v** sound, as in **have**.

The words in the box end with the letters **ve**. Use them to complete the sentences below. You can use the words in the box more than once.

mauve   live   cave   love   give   leave   move

"Ugh! Ugh! I will never _____move_____ away and _____leave_____ my

_____cave_____ !" shouted the huge, scary _____mauve_____ monster.

"I _____love_____ to _____live_____ in this dark _____cave_____

and I _____love_____ to _____give_____ you a FRIGHT!"

Draw a picture of the scary monster. Give him two names that rhyme.

Answers may vary   Answers may vary

18

This page introduces the spelling pattern **ve** for a short **v** sound. Your child fills in the missing words and then draws and names the monster. He or she can use any rhyming words with spelling patterns covered previously.

The "le" ending ★

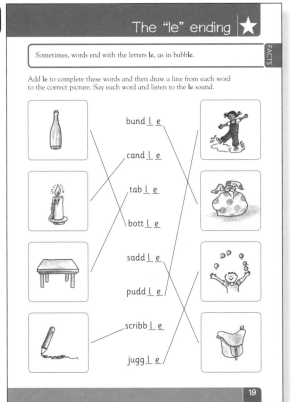

Sometimes, words end with the letters **le**, as in bub**ble**.

Add **le** to complete these words and then draw a line from each word to the correct picture. Say each word and listen to the **le** sound.

bund l e

cand l e

tab l e

bott l e

sadd l e

pudd l e

scribb l e

jugg l e

Encourage your child to say the words with the **le** ending while matching them with the pictures. He or she should look for words with the **le** ending when reading or looking at print in everyday situations.

★ Different letters, same sound

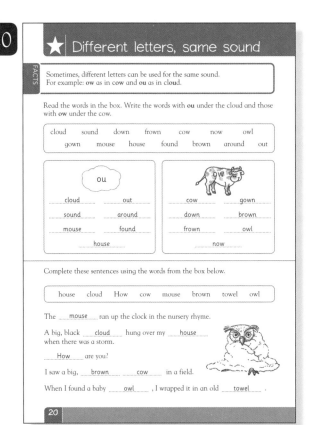

Sometimes, different letters can be used for the same sound. For example: **ow** as in c**ow** and **ou** as in cl**ou**d.

Read the words in the box. Write the words with **ou** under the cloud and those with **ow** under the cow.

cloud   sound   down   frown   cow   now   owl
gown   mouse   house   found   brown   around   out

ou

cloud   out
sound   around
mouse   found
house

ow

cow   gown
down   brown
frown   owl
now

Complete these sentences using the words from the box below.

house   cloud   How   cow   mouse   brown   towel   owl

The _____mouse_____ ran up the clock in the nursery rhyme.

A big, black _____cloud_____ hung over my _____house_____ when there was a storm.

_____How_____ are you?

I saw a big, _____brown_____ _____cow_____ in a field.

When I found a baby _____owl_____ , I wrapped it in an old _____towel_____ .

This page introduces different spelling patterns for the same sound – **ow** as in **cow** and **ou** as in cl**ou**d. Your child has to sort the words into groups with the same spelling patterns. This helps in recognising letter patterns in words.

Suffixes ★

A **suffix** is a group of letters that can be added to the end of a **root word**. For example: **ing**, **er**, **en**, **ed**, **est** and **y** are all suffixes.
Remember: if a word ends in **e**, take it away before you add a suffix.

Add a suffix to each of these root words and write the new word.

smile + ing = _____smiling_____

brave + er = _____braver_____

fine + est = _____finest_____

like + ed = _____liked_____

take + en = _____taken_____

nose + y = _____nosy_____

Complete these sentences. Use the words you have written above.

Ali's cup is finer than Jo's, but my gold cup is the _____finest_____ of all.

I did not like waiting in the queue, but I _____liked_____ the roller coaster.

I hate having to smile for a photo, but I like _____smiling_____ at other times.

Dad told me not to take my new boots to school, but it was too late! I had already _____taken_____ them.

The activity is to make new words using the suffixes **ing**, **er**, **ed**, **est** and **y**, and to then use these words to complete the sentences.

★ Taking away the suffix

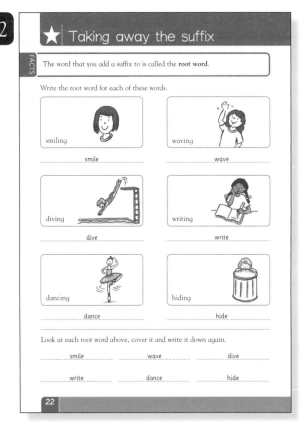

The word that you add a suffix to is called the **root word**.

Write the root word for each of these words.

smiling
_____smile_____

waving
_____wave_____

diving
_____dive_____

writing
_____write_____

dancing
_____dance_____

hiding
_____hide_____

Look at each root word above, cover it and write it down again.

_____smile_____   _____wave_____   _____dive_____

_____write_____   _____dance_____   _____hide_____

The term **root word** is introduced and this time your child has to identify and remove the suffix, leaving the root word. Encourage him or her to practise writing the root words again without copying.

Adding a suffix ★

FACTS

When a **root word** ends in a short vowel and a consonant, **double** the last letter before adding a suffix, such as **ing**, **ed**, **er**, **en**, **est** or **y**.
For example: **hop** + **ing** = **hopping**

Finish these word sums.

shop + ing = ... shopping

slip + ed = ... slipped

fun + y = ... funny

sad + est = ... saddest

fat + en = ... fatten

mud + y = ... muddy

run + ing = ... running

hot + est = ... hottest

sun + y = ... sunny

Here, your child learns to make new words by doubling the last consonant before adding a suffix. Frequent practice is needed to become familiar with words that either drop the **e** or double letters before adding the suffix.

★ Spelling practice

FACTS

Remember: Look   Say   Cover   Write   Check

Can you spell these words?

after	after	bird	bird
many	many	more	more
some	some	home	home
ask	ask	work	work
would	would	open	open
boy	boy	she	she
every	every	may	may
any	any	help	help
best	best	left	left
back	back	these	these

Write the sentences that are read out to you.
Listen, think and then write.

One sunny day, / a little girl / went for / a walk / in the woods. / Behind a tree, / she saw / a little house / and the door / was open. / She went / inside / very slowly. / She could not see / anyone inside, / but a table / was ready / for a meal. / She saw / three bowls, / three cups / and three spoons. / She saw three chairs, / a little one, / a bigger one / and an even / bigger one. / Who do / you think / lived in / this house?

Encourage your child to go through the Look, Say, Cover, Write and Check activity and write the words clearly. Read the dictation above and repeat, pausing at the marks. Your child may be ready to add punctuation.

Is it "ck" or "k"? ★

FACTS

The letters **ck** and **k** are used for the same sound. How do you know which one to use? You have to look at the word and ask yourself, "Does that look right?"

Which word in each pair looks right? Write the correct word on the dotted line.

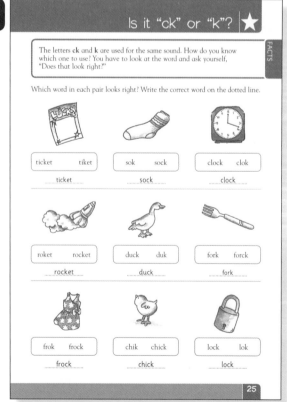

ticket	tiket	sok	sock	clock	clok
ticket		sock		clock	

roket	rocket	duck	duk	fork	forck
rocket		duck		fork	

frok	frock	chik	chick	lock	lok
frock		chick		lock	

This page encourages your child to look carefully at pairs of words with **ck** and **k** endings and decide which word looks right. Extend this activity by playing this game with other words, to encourage your child to check spellings.

★ "k" and "c"

FACTS

The letter **k** always needs the letter **c** to stand between it and a **short vowel** sound, as in **neck**. The letter **k** can stand alone after a **long vowel** sound, as in **like**. It can also stand alone after some consonants, as in **walk**.

Complete these words.

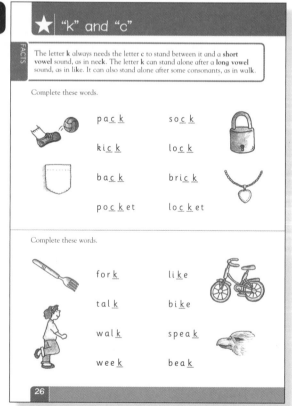

pa<u>c</u> k   so<u>c</u> k

ki<u>c</u> k   lo<u>c</u> k

ba<u>c</u> k   bri<u>c</u> k

po<u>c</u><u>k</u> et   lo<u>c</u><u>k</u> et

Complete these words.

for <u>k</u>   li <u>k</u> e

tal <u>k</u>   bi <u>k</u> e

wal <u>k</u>   spea <u>k</u>

wee <u>k</u>   bea <u>k</u>

For words ending with a **k** sound, use **ck** after a short vowel sound or **k** after a long vowel sound. This activity involves looking at and saying the words carefully. It encourages your child to check spellings and apply spelling rules.

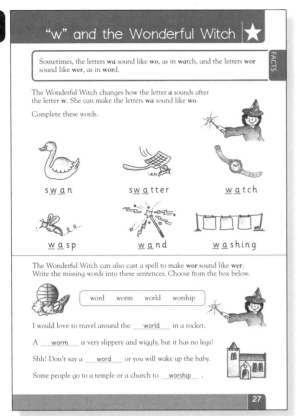

27 "w" and the Wonderful Witch ★

FACTS

Sometimes, the letters **wa** sound like **wo**, as in **wa**tch, and the letters **wor** sound like **wer**, as in **wor**d.

The Wonderful Witch changes how the letter **a** sounds after the letter **w**. She can make the letters **wa** sound like **wo**.

Complete these words.

s w **a** n

sw **a** tter

w **a** tch

w **a** sp

w **a** nd

w **a** shing

The Wonderful Witch can also cast a spell to make **wor** sound like **wer**. Write the missing words into these sentences. Choose from the box below.

| word | worm | world | worship |

I would love to travel around the __world__ in a rocket.

A __worm__ is very slippery and wiggly, but it has no legs!

Shh! Don't say a __word__ or you will wake up the baby.

Some people go to a temple or a church to __worship__ .

27

When **w** is put before a vowel, the vowel sound in a word can change – **wa** becomes a **wo** sound and **wor** becomes a **wer** sound. Encourage your child to say the words aloud while completing this activity.

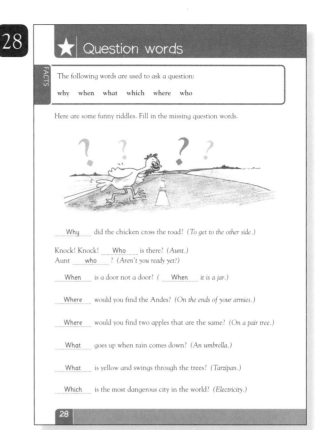

28 ★ Question words

FACTS

The following words are used to ask a question:

why   when   what   which   where   who

Here are some funny riddles. Fill in the missing question words.

____Why____ did the chicken cross the road? *(To get to the other side.)*

Knock! Knock! ____Who____ is there? *(Aunt.)*
Aunt ____who____ ? *(Aren't you ready yet?)*

____When____ is a door not a door? (____When____ it is a jar.)

____Where____ would you find the Andes? *(On the ends of your armies.)*

____Where____ would you find two apples that are the same? *(On a pair tree.)*

____What____ goes up when rain comes down? *(An umbrella.)*

____What____ is yellow and swings through the trees? *(Tarzipan.)*

____Which____ is the most dangerous city in the world? *(Electricity.)*

28

This page introduces question words. Jokes and riddles will help your child select and spell the correct word.

---

29 Don't get in a muddle ★

FACTS

There are many spellings for the sound **air**, as in ch**air**.
For example: **are**, **ere**, **ear** and **air**.

There are many spellings for the **or** sound.
For example: **or**, **oor**, **aw**, **au** and **ore**.

Complete these sentences using the words in the box below.

| chair | there | care | bear |

I sat on a broken __chair__ .

I have a very old teddy __bear__ .

"Go over __there__ ," the teacher said.

Walking in the rain is fun. I don't __care__ if I get wet.

Draw a line joining each word to the correct picture.

door
draw
daughter
claw
snore
saw

29

This page looks at different spellings for the **air** sound and the **or** sound. It is important that as your child learns to spell more words, she or he can easily recall these differing letter combinations.

---

30 ★ More of a muddle

FACTS

Some words that are spelled differently sound the same but mean different things. For example: **which** and **witch** sound the same but have different meanings.

Underline the words in the sentences below that sound the same but don't mean the same thing and then write both words.

I am over <u>here</u>. I couldn't <u>hear</u> you calling.
__here__   __hear__

I can see <u>their</u> coats. They are over <u>there</u>.
__their__   __there__

An elephant has a trunk and <u>two</u> tusks, <u>too</u>.
__two__   __too__

<u>Where</u> are you are going? You can't <u>wear</u> that hat!
__where__   __wear__

How many small words can you make from this large word?

misunderstanding

Answers may vary

30

Your child should know about words that sound the same but are spelled differently and have different meanings (homophones). Making smaller words using the letters in a long word is a fun way to learn to spell.

Colours of the rainbow ★

Colour words and other descriptive words enrich writing skills.

Finish these sentences with the correct colour word.

Roses are .... red ....

The sky is .... blue ....

Corn is .... yellow ....

The grass is .... green ....

I like a nice juicy .... orange ....

Violet is another word for .... purple ....

Night is .... black ....

Snow is .... white ....

A tree trunk is .... brown ....

An elephant is .... grey ....

Colour each of the balloons
using a pen that matches
the colour word inside it.

On this page, your child learns how to spell colour words. Your child should be able to use these colour words and other descriptive words with confidence to enrich his or her independent writing skills.

★ More spelling practice

Remember: Look   Say   Cover   Write   Check

Can you spell these words?

their	their	year	year
there	there	under	under
then	then	woman	woman
where	where	tell	tell
what	what	keep	keep
who	who	sit	sit
them	them	own	own
how	how	let	let
us	us	little	little
yes	yes	which	which

Write the sentences that are read out to you.
Listen, think and then write.

Once upon a time, / there was / a boy / who was / called Jack. /
On Monday, / he went / into town / and sold / his mother's / cow /
for a handful / of beans! / She was / very cross / and threw / them out /
of the window. / On Friday, / Jack looked out / of the window / and saw /
a very / large beanstalk. / It was / so tall / that it almost / reached /
a cloud. What do / you think / happened / next?

Here, your child revises many spellings of words from previous pages. Read the dictation above and then read the passage slowly, pausing at the marks shown. This dictation includes many words and spelling patterns.

Glossary

Consonants
The 21 letters of the alphabet that are not vowels. The letter **y** can be both a vowel (as in **sky**) or a consonant (as in **year**).

Homophones
Words that sound the same but have different spellings and meanings, such as **pear** and **pair**.

Noun
A word for an object, person, place, quality or state. **Harry**, **sadness**, **monkey**, **cheese** and **France** are all examples of nouns.

Plural
More than one of something. We usually (but not always) add an **s** to the end of a singular noun to make it plural. For example: **houses**, **books** and **songs**.

Root word
The form of a word without any suffixes (or prefixes, which come before the root word). For example: **laugh** is the root word of **laughing**.

Singular
Just one of something, such as a **dolphin** or a **flower**.

Suffix
A group of letters added to the end of a root word to change its meaning or how it is used. Examples include **ing** and **ed**, which are common suffixes of verbs.

Verb
A doing, or action, word, such as (to) **run**, **smile** and **sleep**.

Vowels
The letters **a**, **e**, **i**, **o** and **u**. The letter **y** is often used as a vowel, too.